Nine to Five Temptation

Enemies to Steamy Romance

J. D. Hova

J . D . HOVA PUBLISHING
JDH
WHERE IDEAS COME TO LIFE

Table of Contents

1

Katrina's POV

I wake up to the blaring sound of my alarm and sigh, slightly frustrated by the three hours of sleep I managed to get and somewhat excited about what today entails.

The night before was spent with many hours preparing for whatever challenges my new job would throw at me: going over the guidelines and ethics and familiarizing myself with every possible bit of information to get myself prepared to work with the Torrent Exporting Company.

It has been my dream company for years, and I got the job with the high qualifications needed for one to be employed, and luckily I met their standards.

I get up from bed and run my usual morning drill, preparing to leave for work. After having my meal, which is a plate of simple macaroni and cheese, I step out of the house and head towards my car, praying inwardly with crossed fingers that everything goes well today.

During the orientation for the newly employed staff, it had been noted that the boss is unforgiving regarding mistakes or errors, no matter how little the oversight, and someone with any flop would lead to immediate dismissal from employment.

Personally, after listening to everything the staff who had given the orientation said, I thought it was instead a rash policy on the boss's part, given that people are liable to make mistakes. A single mistake shouldn't be used to judge a person's potential.

But then again, this policy is what has gotten the company to the flourishing stage that it is at. So if it is efficient, I must carefully avoid anything implicating me while working.

I get into my car and start the engine, confident of myself because with the extent to which I have prepared for today and the determination to retain my position as an employee; it should all go smoothly.

I am brought out of my thoughts when I hear my phone ringing, look at the caller ID, and see Flora's name on the screen.

A smile comes to my face as I pick up the call, eager to talk to someone familiar before I'm thrown into the vast ocean of strangers whom I have to get acquainted with.

"Hey there." Her chirpy voice reaches me from the other end of the call, and my smile grows; she sounds tired.

"Hey dear," I say to her in a light and cheery voice.

"I'm guessing you are on your way to work right now, tsk-tsk," she says to me, and I can tell she is shaking her head.

"As it's expected of me Flora. You should also be on your way to work," I scold her lightly. Her habit of going late to work might get her in trouble one day.

"Yes mum. That's not why I called anyways, your dad called," She says, and I sigh as I roll my eyes.

"What's the matter this time?" I ask her, knowing I would not like whatever she says next.

"He said that your mum complained that you have not been taking her calls," she says to me, and a frown comes to my face.

My mum's demands are always either ridiculous or demanded at the wrong time, so the best option is to ignore her calls for my peace of mind.

Both my parent's numbers remain blocked until I see the need to reach out to them, so right now, Flora is the only link they have to pass information to me, and thankfully, her mobile phone rarely stays on.

The reason she called would most likely be related to my new job that I had informed both of them about, and then her whining would begin, and it's always the same thing.

"Kat, I never see you anymore."

"I come home when I can."

"Your dad is the only face I see right now."

"Of course."

"You are twenty-six and single, love, what time would you use to get a family of your own if you start working now?"

The last statement has been reoccurring in different forms for the past two years since I left my previous relationship, and she has remained very persistent that I enter a new one.

Her whining usually gives me a headache, so I ignore her and her calls altogether.

"Yeah, and we both know why," I say to her stiffly, already fed up with the discussion.

"Hey girl, don't go switching up on me; all this isn't my fault," she says with her voice slightly raised, and I sigh again.

"I know Flora, but right now, I just don't want to talk about my parents, I'm already tensed up enough because of this new job, the last thing I need is to procure a mental image of my family drama and start work with it," I say to her, and she chuckles.

"Well," she sighs, "I'm sorry, but I have strict orders to inform you of a celebratory dinner at your parent's house by 7 pm, attendance is mandatory," she says, and I can't help but laugh at her statement.

"You and I both know that is not happening," I tell her with all seriousness.

"They can't expect me to return from work on my first day and go to their house for dinner.

"Exactly what I told them, but there is a penalty stated Kat. If you don't attend the dinner this evening, at the break of dawn tomorrow morning your mum will be at your door step ready to spend a week vacation with you," she says to me, amused by my situation, and I groan out loud.

"What the fuck is wrong with these people?" I ask no one in particular, and Flora laughs.

"Sorry hon, but I have to go now. Anyways, good luck on your set up dinner date," she says with humor in her voice as she hangs up the call, and I let out a weak breath, already exhausted from the day.

Dinner with my parents implies that I have to cope with a new different male specimen that my mum selects in a bid to get me into a relationship, hopefully, and each time she does this, the night always ends with me wanting to wring the necks of my imposed dates.

I get that I am their only child, and they expect a whole lot from me, but really, their persistent nature and various creative ways to get to me are mentally draining.

My mum insists that I am too ambitious and, as a lady, I shouldn't put this much effort into working but instead into finding a good and successful man to marry.

There was a time I bought this entire idea, I gave up all my ambitions to support a man, and I had stupidly let myself mistake comfort for love, fleeting laughter for happiness, and pain as a criterion for pleasure.

But that made me end up broken and scarred to date.

I battled with the psychological implication of my past relationship for an entire year, and it took another year to get myself back on my feet.

As I reach my destination, I break out of my thoughts, not seeing the point in bringing back painful memories. I am not as foolish as I was two years ago; as they say, experience is the best teacher.

After parking my car, I switch off my engine and step down, taking continuous deep breaths and trying to summon back my courage that withered due to my train of thoughts earlier.

I walk into the building, and as expected, it's already filled up with employees going about their business.

"Miss Katrina Field?" A lady dressed in a black suit approaches me.

"Yes, that's me," I say to her with a polite smile which she returns.

"Come with me, please," she says as she walks towards an elevator in haste. I follow her into it, and we stand silently approaching the last floor.

"This is your office," She says to me, pointing at a door with my name tagged on it. "My office is right across yours if you have any questions." She finishes.

"Thank you, Miss Stephen," I say politely, reading her name tag on the door and she smiles and turns to leave but pauses as suddenly due to the office in front of both of ours opens up, and a man also dressed in an immaculate black suit steps out looking extremely irritated.

There is no mistaking the authority, his strides portray it, and it doesn't take much to realize that he is the boss, even without being told.

He stops walking when he sees us and his eyes land on me as he takes in my appearance, not giving off any reaction, only making me feel self-conscious.

For ten seconds, I zone out and run my eyes over him, taking in every detail, from his ebony black hair to his grey eyes and pink lips to his well-tailored suit that could barely contain his very appealing muscles underneath it.

I give myself a mental shake and scold myself inwardly for having such thoughts.

"Miss Stephen, you are fired," he says calmly to the lady beside me, bringing me out of my daze, gasping in shock, and watching the smile on the lady's face drop.

Well, that confirms that he's the boss.

"I'm sorry sir?" The lady asks, stuttering slightly as the color drains from her face.

"You heard me *clearly,* Miss Stephen, get your things together and submit your resignation letter on my desk by tomorrow," he says to her, and she stands there speechless for a moment.

"But sir," she starts saying, but he cuts her short.

"It would be in your own best interest if you refrain from saying any other word. I don't tolerate carelessness and you have proven more than once to be incompetent," he scolds her coldly.

I catch drops of tears rolling down her eyes, which she quickly wipes and nods her head in response before walking away quickly into her office.

I look back at the male, who looks unaffected by what just happened, and I see his eyes now focused on me.

I can't help but feel angered by his action; that was a very rude and absolutely unnecessary way to let go of staff; at the very least, he should have had the decency to call her into his office to fire her.

"What position did your employment state?" he asks me, running his eyes over me slowly, and I feel my body warm up under his gaze, much to my dislike.

He looks up to see the tag on my office door stating my position in the company.

"Close enough," he says, not waiting for my reply, "you must have the qualifications, I'm sure you can handle the position of a secretary," he states rather than asking me, with a serious tone, as he turns and walks away, not giving me the chance to say a single word.

I stand on the spot, surprised by the fact that he just decided to hand over his secretary's position to me and also the extent of arrogance his appealing appearance encompasses.

Suddenly working here doesn't feel as exciting as before I met him; if letting go of his staff is that easy for him, then there is no assurance that I would not be let go just as easily.

It will be a serious issue if I have to put up with this attitude each day.

The silent smile on his face and the look in his eyes shows that, just like every other male, he has a motive behind this promotion, and I will be damned if I let him have his way.

"Miss Field, tell Miss Stephen to get you up to speed with all you are expected to do before she leaves if she wants her final pay," He says to me before entering his office and shuts the door.

This is mind-boggling.

2

NICK'S POV

"I'll be around for the next hour, so you can come over," I say to Christian over the phone as I start rounding up work for the day.

It is typical for him to want to come to work thirty minutes before my closing time. Christian happens to be the kind of billionaire with no stress on his plate, taking life easy and getting everything he needs.

He also happens to be my senior brother, the CEO of my company.

Being the CEO of this company, he practically reaps the fruit of my labor, not ever showing interest in the company but only interested in the money he gets from it.

Knowing his irresponsible lifestyle, our father, for the sake of his position as the firstborn son, stated in his will that he is to run the company as the CEO for three years. Afterward, if he shows any sign of seriousness to the welfare of the company, then he would retain the position permanently.

He also stated that I am to be his manager and watch his progress or lack of it, ensuring that the company doesn't fall into ruins.

Once his stipulated three years reach and he fails, I will take over the company CEO position.

I've tried to talk him into being serious with his position severally and stop being immature, but all he ever seems to care about is how much he gets to have each week.

He has been like this for the past two years, and I've kept things running smoothly in the company.

"Sir, the paper work for 'Taylor's Gem' needs your signature, I have already gone through all the details and they are accurate," Katrina says to me as she steps into my office, bringing me out of my thoughts.

I take in her appearance, which never fails to dazzle me with her very appealing figure, from her hazel brown hair to her enchanting big blue eyes, to her lovely smile which only graces her face rarely, most times when she is not around me, to her attractive figure, and her fullness in all the right places.

Her body is an hourglass made for perfection, complimenting everything about her. Her tiny waist just highlights her features, making her irresistibly appealing to the sight.

She certainly does not fail to bring wild thoughts to my mind. Cooking up all the sinful things I could do to her body when she is not clothed. Sometimes, I hate it; she is a distraction.

The unique thing about her is that, unlike other women who want to use their bodies to gain favor, it's the opposite for her, as she finds every possible reason not to get closer than three feet to me. If my observation is accurate, which it always is, she seems to have great antipathy towards me, for reasons beyond me.

For a professional working relationship, I push my curiosity about why she dislikes me to the side and just admire her secretly, for now.

"Place them on the table Katrina, I'll go over them again before signing," I say to her before averting my gaze from her and focusing back on my laptop.

"There is something else, sir," she says to me as she drops the documents on my table, and I notice that she has her laptop in her hands.

"Okay, what is it?" I ask her, and she places the laptop in front of me and turns it to face me.

"The proposed net margin of 'Thriller Costumes' is not adding up with our record," she says to me, still standing across the table and pointing towards the screen facing me.

"I believe your explanation would be much better if you come over here and point it out for me," I say to her, giving her a pointed look with a nonchalant voice as I pull her laptop closer to myself, urging her to turn around the table to my side.

For a second, I see a guarded, suspicious look on her face which she masks before finally deciding to turn and stand beside me.

"Better. Now, show me what's wrong," I say to her, and she bends slightly but is still very wary of making any physical contact with me as she ensures that there is enough space between us, and I can't help but smirk inwardly.

The closeness, though, is enough for me to catch a whiff of her perfume that scents like lavender which suits her perfectly.

I listen with rapt attention to every explanation she gives, making sure to not make any moves that would make her uncomfortable.

For the past three weeks, she has been on her guard, doing everything perfectly and learning and coping with her new position quickly. Still, a good working relationship is built on trust, and she needs to be comfortable around me enough to trust me.

"The fault is most likely from the first record of export, recheck that," I say to her after she is done with her thorough explanation.

She turns and looks at me with a smile that I'm sure she didn't give consciously, it probably came from the relief she felt at the solution she just got, but this didn't stop me from returning her smile.

"Thank you, sir," She says to me as she stands straight and hurriedly turns to leave, seeming eager to make the corrections and be done for the day.

"Katrina," I call out her name, stopping her movement, and she turns and faces me with a questioning look.

"You forgot this," I say as I point to the laptop she left on my table.

I watch as a blush comes to her face as realization dawns on her that she forgot to retrieve her laptop, and I can't help the smirk that comes to my face at her reaction.

It is at brief moments like this, little slip-ups that let me know that I am not the only one affected by this sizzling attraction between us.

It's somewhat relieving that underneath that thick coat of dislike she has towards me, there is still a part of her that loses focus when she is around me, which brings me great pleasure.

And I would really love to see all of her lose focus as lust clouds her senses when I have her writhing in pleasure under me.

"Thank you, again," She says quietly as she picks up the laptop and turns to leave.

I nod in reply to her, and I watch her hips sway as she walks the short distance between my table and the door.

Considering what a great temptress she is, with the very innocent and mundane things that she does, it's a thing of pride that I have not gone against my work ethic for the past three weeks and had my way with her.

I'm about to go back to finishing up for the day, but I get distracted by the sound of Christian and Katrina bumping against each other as she opens the door.

"Ouch!" she exclaims as Christian steadies her with his hands.

"Are you okay?" I and Christian ask simultaneously, and I stand up and move towards them as Christian still examines her with his eyes as I get close to her to do the same.

"Yeah, I'm fine," she says with a quiet voice as blood rushes up to her cheeks and ears because of how close Christian and I are to her, and she tries to avert her gaze from both of us.

"Well, this is a terrible way to meet," Christian says with humor in his voice as he runs his eyes over her, and she looks up at him and chuckles at his statement, pushing a strand of hair behind her ear.

"I'm Christian, CEO of this company," he says, not failing to flaunt his status in the sentence he says to her, and I shoot him an unimpressed look before returning to my seat.

"I'm Katrina, secretary of this company," she says with a

chuckle, obviously amused by his introduction, and I glare at both of them as their hands linger in a handshake that neither seems to want to end.

"That's lovely," He says simply in reply keeping his gaze locked on her, and I see her blush intensify as she keeps a flirtatious smile on her face.

I feel annoyed at her reaction to him; one would think she would at least have the decency to flirt with him when she is not standing right before me.

This just proves that I was greatly mistaken about my opinion of her; she didn't need the company's manager's attention but rather chose to target the CEO, seeing that he was the best bet to gain favor in the company.

"That will be all, Miss Field," I say to her coldly, not bothering to hide my displeasure.

She turns and looks at me, reading my reaction and giving me a strange look before nodding and walking out of the office, but not before smiling at Christian again.

"Well isn't she pretty?" He says to me with a huge smirk on his face as he takes a seat.

I don't bother replying to him as my mind replays everything that just happened and focuses solely on Katrina's expression.

To think I thought she was different, with her guarded smile, crystal clear and innocent eyes, strict professional charisma, and unexplained strong dislike towards me.

It had all been a ruse to hide who she was, and I was clouded enough to fall for it.

Just like other ladies, she prefers the shortcut of making use of her womanly charms to gain favor rather than the hardworking and dedicated lady she portrays daily before me.

At least she has higher standards than others who had desperately tried to get me in between their legs; she has a much higher target; rather than go after a mere company manager, she sought to go after the big dog who owns it all.

I can't help but feel angry at myself for falling for her act and thinking she is any better; I should have seen through it all.

I had even gone to admiring her on a rather personal level than a professional one.

What annoys me even more is that, right now, with the knowledge that she might likely be a qualified and well-experienced gold digger, I still feel extremely attracted to her.

"Another conquest for your taking, I believe," I say finally to Christian, and the mere thought of the actualization of my statement irritates me.

"Fingers crossed, she might just be," he says with a cocky smile that screams his excitement at finding a new lay.

She might just be.

The next day, she still carries her *oh-so-innocent* and morally upright attitude while working, as if she didn't give Christian a silent but not-so-subtle invitation yesterday.

But unlike other days, she seems rather comfortable around me, suspiciously.

I guess since she got the attention of whom she wanted, she doesn't have to put on a full 100% show for me anymore.

As much as I would love to say that this new change of hers is repulsive in every right, that would be nothing but a lie because each warm smile she gives, the still innocent and breathtaking look in her eyes, her calm demeanor, and her not so secret glances at me that comes with a faint blush when caught, just seems to gradually melt the cold exterior that I had spent all night building.

I still want to see those innocent eyes clouded in a lustful haze and that composed demeanor shattered as she screams out my name, her body riding on the height of pleasure.

To crown it all, she goes about her day oblivious to her effect on me and the mental images she initiates daily, creating fantasies of pure sin that disrupt my always-composed mental state.

If she can get me this riled up without physical contact, then she is a pretty good actress and deserves accolades for her exceptional job.

As for now, I will go along with this ruse until she gets what she wants and, just like every other gold digger, leaves for good.

As long as she maintains and keeps on working to perfection, we will not have any issues, and it will be a professional working relationship between us, as it is expected to be; her personal life and who she decides to entice or flirt with is none of my business.

But as factual as all those are, ignoring these disturbing attractions towards her would not be easy, especially if she keeps looking at me with these soul-searching eyes every time she says 'good morning' to me.

3

WORK PROJECTS

*S*oul-crushing, *heart-wrenching,* and ears bleeding minutes pass as my mum narrates several reasons why she got married at an early age and why I should emulate her.

I had called her to ask if there would be a Christmas party this year and now I regret it.

"I have to go now mum, I'll be late for work," I say to her, interrupting her lecture and hang up, not waiting for her to reply.

I had gotten my answer and had also found out that she and Dad were doing very fine since the last time we spoke.

Thankfully, as much as I am sure she will try, she will not be able to call me. It's a new week in December and also winter, my least favorite season of the year.

It's my fourth week at work, and let's just say I'm pretty proud that I have lasted that long.

I happen to be one secretary that has lasted more than three weeks in the company, in a very long time, so I was told by few of my colleagues.

I had hoped that winter would take a little while longer before coming, but just like each year, the snow takes me by surprise, and I find myself already wearing coats and hand gloves, which can be very tiring to put on each day to work.

I'm currently on my way to work, driving through light snowfall that signifies that this year's snow would not be very pleasant and more dreadful than last year's.

Here in Chicago, one would expect that the snow would start on the third week of December, but rather, this year just has to be one of those years that it starts on the first week and slowly and steadily increases in vigor, making every single thing more difficult for one to do.

I could go on and list numerous things winter puts a stop to, but that would be mentally draining and would also ruin what's left of my good mood since the phone call with my mum.

I reach my workplace and step out of the car, into the building, readying myself for a hectic day at work and also prepping myself for more hectic days to come.

Not to add that the cold and heavy coat doesn't help in any way.

I step into the building to see it busier than ever, which doesn't surprise me, considering the number of emails I received throughout the weekend, from various sectors, concerning various goods in demand that needs immediate verification before exportation.

During this festive period, most companies get more demand

for their products, based on the fact that everyone just needs to get new things during winter as gifts for their families, even though the prices of various goods increase significantly during this time.

This is also one of the reasons I dislike winter, the extravagant spending.

I exchange greetings with some staff as I head to the elevator, ready for my tripled workload today due to the beginning of this horrible winter season.

Deep down, I know that all these reasons are just meager facts that I brought up to hide the real fact about why I really hate winter.

I had my heart broken this season, two days before Christmas to be précised, and it completely crushed my festive spirit and whatever made winter endearing to me.

Not that I would admit that to myself right now; for all I know, the extra workload I have on my plate is more than enough to make me detest this season.

I step out of the elevator, and I'm met by Mr. Nickolas Cross, manager of Torrent's company, also my smoking hot boss, all dressed immaculately in a well-tailored suit, as usual, to entice in a subtle manner.

"Good morning, sir," I say to him, breaking out of my thoughts as I step out of the elevator.

He reads my expression for a brief moment, taking in my appearance, and I watch his reactions as he sees me for the first time in winter clothes, and I wonder why he doesn't have any warm clothes on as well.

He runs his eyes from my thick coat down to my boots and maintains a stoic and expressionless face.

"Good morning, Miss Field. I hope you had a good weekend?" he asks me, still staring at me deeply, which unnerves me as usual.

"Yes sir," I say to him, not letting the commotion he is causing within me with just his gaze show on my appearance as I keep a polite smile on my face.

"Well then, you came right on time, we have a bunch of meetings to attend at different companies today, and I'm glad you are dressed for the occasion," He says to me with a serious tone and I stare at him shocked.

"But sir, I have a lot of work to do here, and besides I only just got here," I say to him, not understanding why he cannot just go to the meetings on his own like other times.

"It's not up for debate, Miss Field, these are very important meetings based on projects we have to carry out within a short time span, between now and the 23rd of this month when everywhere and everything will be shut down."

"I'll give you ten minutes to get yourself ready and meet me by my car," he finalizes, not leaving room for any further complaints, and punches the elevator button, ultimately ending the discussion.

Not left with any other choice, I reluctantly walk towards my office and drop my bag, not feeling so good that I still have to wear the boots and coat that I had looked forward to removing once I got inside.

I turn hot coffee from the coffee pot into a plastic cup, turning in enough milk and a little bit of sugar; I stir it and shut the lid of the cup.

I take out my iPad from my bag and take a sip of my coffee before stepping out of the office, feeling prepared and ready to dive right back into the cold.

I go down the elevator and out of the building to the car park, and I immediately spot Nick's black Ferrari and walk towards it.

Reaching it, I get into the car, sitting in the backseat beside him. Once I'm settled inside, the driver immediately starts the car and drives off.

I ensure to keep enough distance between me and Nick, who casts a side glance at the distance between us but doesn't react as usual.

For the past weeks, he has proven to be the exact opposite of the pervert I suspected he was, though the arrogance I observed is very accurate and has been portrayed on various occasions to both me and other staff.

He has been nothing but the typical arrogant and strict boss he was rumored to be and hasn't shown any iota of disrespect to me or even attempted to do so.

Up till last week, he used to be a charming, smart, and sometimes funny boss, but he still maintained his strict business principle, and this attitude of his made me loosen up slowly, even with my suspicion that he put me in this position I am in for the wrong reasons.

Last week though, he seemed a lot colder, he limited his smile and kept an extra strict persona, for which I have no idea why.

And as much as I would not admit it to myself, it stung a little that when I had become more comfortable around him, he decided to keep on an unapproachable vibe.

I focus on sipping my coffee quietly as Nick remains on a call, which sounds pretty serious based on his no-nonsense tone.

He remains on the call till we reach our first destination, which is a hotel, to my surprise.

The car stops, and he steps down; not wasting a second, I get down, following him and trying to keep up with his hurried pace.

We both get into the hotel, and he makes a beeline for a lady seated at a table in the corner, and I follow him silently.

"Cynthia," He calls out with a smile, and I note the lack of an official title as he says her name.

The lady in a black body-fitted gown smiles at him and stands up to hug him.

"Nickolas," She says in delight as they both hug each other in familiarity.

"It's been a long time," He says to her, still maintaining his smile, and for a moment, I feel like a third wheel.

"Yeah it has, please sit," She says to both me and him.

"This must be your secretary," she says to him as she stretches out her hand for a handshake which I take with a polite smile plastered on my face.

"Yes, she is," he says simply in reply.

"I had not expected you to be working for Miles company," he says to her, and I feel myself ease up at the mention of the Android Production Company; I had started to think that he brought me here to supervise his date.

"Well, we both knew things weren't going to work out with me still being your secretary," The female says with a teasing smile and a knowing look, and this chases away my former relief.

A reunion of long-time lovers, is that what this is?

"Yeah, I guess you are right," he says, sending her a sexy smirk, and I feel a strange feeling sprout inside me, one that I choose to acknowledge as disgust. "On to business then, what are the details of the brand and how exactly does your company want the export carried out?" He asks her.

I completely zone out of their conversation and think of how wrong I had been and also very hasty to dismiss my suspicion of him having ulterior motives with me as his secretary, besides it seems to have happened before.

"Did you take down all she said?" Mr. Cross asked, bringing me out of my thoughts, and then I realized that I had not heard a single thing they had said.

He stares at me with clear disappointment in his eyes and only looks away when 'His Jezebel' laughs.

"I guess she must have a lot on her mind, I don't mind running over it again," Cynthia says with a friendly smile.

"Thank you," I say to her when she finishes going over all she said at first again and I jot it down.

With this, we left the hotel, but not after Nick had given her another hug and whispered something into her ear that made her laugh.

The rest of the meetings passed in a hasty blur, and luckily, we didn't meet more 'Jezebel's.'

As much as I hated the first meeting we attended, I must say I learned a great deal from each meeting I attended, and I'm really grateful I went along with him.

The meetings with different companies gave a deeper insight into what the exporting company is all about; meeting equally brilliant CEOs, managers, and secretaries really threw a broader light on how things are run, not just based on the details alone.

The entire mini-trip was eye-opening and more, even thrilling, as after each meeting, Nick made it a point of duty to broadly explain everything that was said and done and also left room for further ideas from me; I would say that he practically molded and broadened my train of thoughts concerning the business and he did so expertly well.

Minus my still very existent dislike for his work ethic to some extent, I must admit, he really is a smart boss.

We both step down from the car, having finished with all meetings for the day and practically finalizing all the hard and tactical parts of each project.

"Good job today, Miss Field," He says to me, and I smile, feeling a sense of pride at his praise.

"Thank you, sir," I say to him and start walking towards the company building, feeling all fluttery and not paying attention to where I am going until I feel an arm wrap itself around me and pull me back with force and great speed.

Just in time, too, because a car speedily drives past me from the car park, not even bothering to horn in warning, and I was too lost in my daze to notice it driving out.

"Who the hell was that?" I hear Nick ask, still not removing his arm from around me and all the initial shock from almost being run over by a car flees from my mind, and all I can focus on is his scent and the masculine heat radiating off him at how close we are.

4

NICK'S POV

$\mathcal{I}$ feel Katrina stiffen in my arms as I pull her to myself speedily.

"Who the hell was that?" I ask no one in particular, angry and wondering if such a person works in my company because if he or she does, that automatically deserves a serious query.

Removing my focus from the already sped-off car, I feel Katrina go lax in my arms as she leans into me, seeming comfortable with my hold on her.

I feel her staring up at me, so I look down and meet her gaze, and the look in her light and clear blue eyes makes my eyes soften, for once I see deeper than she lets on, under the strong, confident personality that she portrays, there is a deep sense of vulnerability, and more.

If I'm not mistaken, deep down underneath her touch-girl act, I see a very lonely beautiful woman, and for once since I met her, she completely let her guard down as she stared at me with longing.

Her eyes seem to stare deeply, searching, peering deep within me before going down to my lips.

Still holding her firmly in my arms, I feel an intense urge to kiss her, to feel those soft-looking pale pink lips on mine, and at this instant, I know she would not resist.

'So what is holding you back?' my subconscious asks me.

I dip my head lower until my face is an inch away from hers and our lips even closer, almost touching.

"We should get inside," I whisper lightly to her instead of fulfilling my desires, and this seems to break the trance between both of us.

"Yes, you're right," She says as she quickly disengages her body from my hold as if suddenly my skin is made of hot coal, and I sigh inwardly.

I watch as she walks hurriedly towards the building, fisting the sides of her coat with her gloved hands.

I had wondered why she went in full winter dress code mood when the cold was barely here.

I smile at how cute she looks in the outfit, regardless.

I start walking towards the building when I see that she has already gone in. I walk into the building and move towards the elevator, and I find her standing there, looking desperate for the elevator to open up.

I stand beside her and feel her tense up, feeling my presence without even looking at me.

The elevator dings and other staff step out of it, leaving way for both of us to enter.

We both stand in the elevator beside each other quietly, but unlike other times, she doesn't keep an enormous distance between us, though the tension in the air is thicker than ever; the sexual energy just sizzles but is not regarded, as we both choose to ignore it.

I can still see how rigid she is as we both wait to reach our destination.

She clears her throat suddenly but still doesn't look at me.

"Thank you for saving me back there," she says to me in a quiet voice, and this surprises me but also puts a smile on my face.

"Well, I couldn't just let you die a few weeks to Christmas now, could I?" I ask her with a smirk, trying to lighten up the mood and ease the tension, and she chuckles finally, turning to look at me.

"I don't think I would have died, sir," she says to me with humor in her voice, and my smirk turns into an amused smile.

I choose to ignore the effect her voice has on me being this close to her, and I focus solely on maintaining a friendly conversation.

"Did you see the speed that car used?" I ask her, keeping a very serious voice but hinting at playfulness, and I see as she tries to hide her smile and feign seriousness too.

"I still don't think that's enough to kill me, I am pretty tough if you must know," She says to me, also amused by my playfulness.

"I would think so, with your very prominent and well-rounded curves, one should expect that toughness from you considering you maintain this exquisite shape by working out daily, or am I wrong?" I ask her and mentally slap myself when all the words leave my mouth, thinking of where that blunt question came from when I'm supposed to be keeping the conversation strictly friendly.

I see a slight blush come to her face as her blue eyes glimmer, and this puts me somewhat at ease that she didn't feel insulted by my stupid misplaced statement.

"That's absolutely right sir, so no speeding car can be the end of me, that would be a waste of my effort in keeping these curves," she says to me with a teasing smile as she stares directly at my eyes, and I smirk at her boldness, I had expected her to change the subject.

'You are treading on dangerous grounds.' My subconscious reminds me.

"And we definitely would not want those curves to go to waste now, would we?" I ask her, sounding humorous but not breaking eye contact and dropping my voice to a husky note, still going on with the teasing.

"I don't think we will sir," she says to me, and I might be fooling myself, but there was a secret, unsaid message just passed now.

Just as I am about to reply to her, the elevator dings, and our brief chat, which was going in a rather sexual direction, is interrupted as we both step out.

My mind started running over everything I said wrong and how unprofessional I sounded, but I completely shut it out.

"Miss Field," I call her as she walks towards her office.

"Yes Sir?" she asks, halting her tracks.

"Feel free to call me when you need saving, anytime, I'll always come to the rescue," I say to her with a teasing voice and a smirk on my face.

"Sir, you make being in danger sound enticing, I must say," She says to me, and once again, I am shocked by her boldness and the fact that she didn't falter as she walks even closer to me with a flirtatious glint in her eyes.

Even as much as I know ending this conversation would be the right thing to do, I am entranced by the very sexy smile on her face. I stand still, and she keeps walking closer to me.

"If it involves me playing, knight in shining armor, then I think you should be in danger often," I say to her, also walking closer to her at this point, or bodies are really close and touching lightly as I stare into her eyes and see the same want that I am sure my eyes mirror.

This time, all sense of proper reasoning evades me, and with a finger, I lift her face up and drop mine slowly until our lips touch each other.

At first, it goes light until she stands on her tiptoes and deepens the kiss, putting her hand around my neck, but immediately she does this, a ding is heard from the elevator, interrupting us.

We quickly readjust ourselves, and she puts distance between us before the person steps out from the elevator.

Looking flushed and surprised at herself, she turns and walks towards her office hurriedly.

I stand at the spot for a while and ponder on what I just did.

How an attempt to save her from getting hit by a car turned into the igniter to the flame I previously kept under control.

It's like that invisible wall that demarcated decency, sensuality, and appropriateness got broken down once I gazed into her eyes and saw the same longing I feel for her in them.

It's like that scenario was the confirmation I needed to advance on her.

Which is absolutely bizarre? Considering all my strong dislike for her flirting with my brother, I shouldn't have easily let my senses be seduced by her.

To think that this led to me kissing her in the hallway where any worker could have easily seen us, not to add that it is improper and unprofessional for a boss and his employee to be involved in such acts.

All the admonitions and reprimands flood my mind as I take slow steps into my office, feeling disappointed in myself that as much as I know all these things, I don't regret kissing her, but rather, my only regret is that it happened in the hallway.

I feel annoyed at myself that no matter how much I beat myself up that what happened is not right, I cannot help but yearn to feel those soft lips on mine again, and this time not in a fleeting kiss.

I walk into my office and sit down, pushing all thoughts of her out of my mind with difficulty as I try to focus on the work in front of me.

Getting engrossed in work for hours, I fail to notice that it's already closing time until I hear a knock on my door.

"It's open," I say, not looking up from the work I am doing.

"I've finalized the accounts I got from other sectors, here they are," Katrina says to me with a stiff tone, and I look up, resting my gaze on her.

"Place them on the table and have a seat Miss Field, we need to talk," I say to her as I pause what I'm doing.

Between my work hours, I had quick and direct mental lashing, and I came up with a suitable solution to handle I and Katrina's situation.

"I'm all ears, sir," she says to me with a composed and unaffected look but is betrayed by her voice which drops a little bit lower than it was when she stepped in.

"Miss Field, I'm sure you are well aware that what happened today is highly inappropriate," I say to her and watch as her composed mask falters a little.

"Yes," she says simply, dropping her voice a little lower but still keeping her head straight and looking all poised and unaffected.

"And you know that such an act could lead to you losing your job immediately," I say to her and watch as worry flashes through her eyes.

"Yes," she replies again stiffly, and I sigh before continuing.

"But we both know that we both initiated it, so the fault is also mine," I say, and to this, she perks up.

Even with the thick tension between and the unpleasant energy, I have the strong urge to turn over the table and take her in my arms again and kiss her senseless.

"But it cannot happen again, it was unprofessional and it is completely unaccepted in a proper office environment," I say to her sternly, and she nods.

"I understand," she says, and rather than feel completely relieved to have this out of the way, a part of me feels disappointed that she did not protest but rather accepted willingly.

"Since that is ironed out, that will be all, Katrina," I say to her dismissively and she stands up.

"Goodnight, Nickolas," she says to me just before opening the door and walking out hurriedly.

I stared at the door that she had just left, still hung up on the fact that she had just said my name for the first time to my hearing, and she didn't seem to have noticed it.

The sultry way in which she just said it broke the dam of logical reasoning, and wild thoughts of several pleasurable instances that she could say my name floods my mind.

Ignoring these already ignited flames of pure attraction would be as hard as a dog ignoring his fetched ball when thrown. Damn!

5

CLOSE CALL

KATRINA'S POV

$\mathcal{A}$fter tossing and turning for good thirty minutes without being able to fall asleep, I lay down, facing the ceiling, and let my thoughts finally focus on all the reasons my sleep is being hindered.

NICKOLAS CROSS.

I could swear I saw a hesitant look in his eyes when he warned that we should put an end to the little unexplained attraction that bloomed within us today.

I had agreed instantly because, as things are, it would be to my own detriment, and plus and minus every sexual tension, I love my job, and I like working with him, and I would love to keep my job.

But the hesitant look I saw in his eyes is what is keeping me up till this time, the thought that I saw his resolve falter as he gave the warning, looking like he wanted the exact opposite of what he was saying.

I have tried for hours to deny that I misinterpreted the look in his eyes because I need to sleep, considering that I have work at 8am tomorrow, but try as I might, I can't deny what I had seen.

That look in his eyes had made something crystal clear; he didn't want it to end as much as I didn't also.

I groan out loud at my train of thoughts, feeling irritated that I even have them, to think I am this attracted to a man I had sought to distance myself from, a man that I believe to be a pervert, a man that proved today that having a fling with his secretary is just as normal and as random as taking coffee daily.

I feel disgust bubble in the pit of my stomach as I remember the warm and sexy look in his eyes when he was talking to his former secretary, one of his many conquests.

No woman should ever stoop so low to settle for a fling with her boss; at least she should have the decency and moral intellect to know that it is wrong and demeaning in a sense.

Then why do I so much want to be in his arms right now?

I groan again, frustrated by the conflict of my emotions, the battle between right, good, and proper, against wants, needs, and desires.

Conveniently, my mind throws in more reasons for sleep to evade me.

My thoughts go back to the conversation in the elevator and how timber-like his voice sounded as he threw in light teasing into our conversation.

How affected I was by mere words of compliments of my figure.

Or maybe that's not what got to me; maybe it's that needy glint

I saw as his grey eyes darkened underneath the teasing look he was portraying as he said the words, '*well rounded curves.*'

I groan out loud again that even from just thinking about him saying it, I just got tingles down my spine.

The tension in the elevator had been palpable, and I had to put on my full restrain to resist the urge of pulling him by the collar and kissing him, throwing caution into the wind.

Luckily the elevator opening up reined those urges a bit until he just had to reignite them.

My thoughts drifted to when he made that statement, '*call me anytime you need saving,*' and how I swooned when he said that, how he made simple words sound so exotic and erotic in my mind.

I remember moving towards him, under a trance, and till now, I don't know where I got the courage to approach him that way, feeling like a predator.

Maybe, it was the all accommodating look in his deep grey eyes that told me he liked that side of me that fueled the sensual movement of my steps.

And then, when he kissed me so lightly, light as a feather's touch, as if testing the waters, it broke the remaining restraint I had, and all I wanted was to deepen the kiss and feel him dive even deeper into insanity.

I sighed at the bliss I felt when I did it until we got interrupted, and at that time, it was like the spell cast on me got broken, and everything I did came crashing through my mind at an overwhelming speed.

I tried so hard to will my thoughts to forget it all and focus on work.

But as hard as I tried to forget it ever happened, I could feel an invisible imprint of his lips on mine, and I can still feel it even now.

And as much as I know it's wrong to admit this, I want so much more than a simple kiss.

I woke up the next morning, not realizing when I had finally been able to fall asleep amidst all my morally conflicting thoughts.

Pushing everything at the back of my mind, I prepare for a new day.

I get into my car and drive, heading to work, and very slowly, I feel my nerves rise at the thought of seeing him again.

How exactly am I supposed to ignore everything I'm feeling when he has crowded my thoughts and invaded my dreams throughout yesterday?

With an addition that those dreams were not as innocent as a simple kiss but far more sensual.

How am I supposed to look him in the eyes and forget that those same eyes had peered at me with hunger in them?

How does he expect me to listen to words that came out from those lips that I kissed yesterday?

'Figure it out.' My subconscious says sternly, and I sigh at the weighty task I have to carry out.

I look at the still mild falling of snow, and my mind goes back to my past relationship.

It's been two years since I felt this sexual drive for any man; I didn't even know I was ready to feel such a drive, considering that I was used and abused mentally and physically by my ex.

I had shut everyone out and solely focused on healing my emotional wounds, not even considering or needing to be with any other person.

Lucas, my ex, had been enough reason for me to completely despise the existence of men.

I didn't expect to start feeling this rush of sexual sensations or even any form of attraction towards a male this soon.

I had initially believed that I would be scarred for life, but all it took for Nick to bring me out of that mental and physical bondage, was just flirtatious smiles that made my stomach flutter and a lingering look that unnerved me, making me self-aware, and also at the same time gives me a boost of feminine confidence, which is something Lucas never did.

'It shouldn't be so hard, right? Just avoid any triggering situation,' I say to myself out loud, thinking about it logically about my situation at hand, I definitely don't want to be one of Nick's conquests, an easy lay for him, I'm definitely more than that.

And on this note, I will just have to ignore this pesky feeling of attraction towards him; the last thing I need is to lose my job, all because of a crush that most likely comes from two years of celibacy.

Besides, anyone with eyes would see that he is an attractive man, and it is very possible to get his physical looks and nothing else, which should be very easy to get rid of.

I get down from my car as I reach my destination, and I walk into the building, greeting others as usual and heading straight for the elevator, still holding on tightly to my logical reasoning and strongly relying on it to suffice once I reach the top floor.

I step out of the elevator as I reach the top floor, and thankfully, this time, I don't meet him standing there.

I make a beeline to my office, not bothering to go to his office and greet him, announcing my presence, just like other days.

I get into the office and take off my gloves, coat, and boot; feeling like a weight has been lifted off my shoulders.

I turn in hot coffee into a mug, prepare it as usual and sit down to begin work, sipping it slowly.

After working for hours and having finished four cups of coffee, I stand up to pour my fifth one when my work phone starts ringing.

I look at the number and realize that it's from Nick's office.

Gulping down my anxiety that suddenly grows, I pick up the phone.

"Hello sir," I greet, extremely thankful that my voice sounds steady and composed, unlike the nervous mess I am right now.

"Miss Field, my office, now," he says into the phone, and I gulp again at the awfully calm tone he speaks with.

"Ok sir," I say as I place the phone back down.

I pour the already-warm coffee into the cup and immediately down it in one gulp.

During my walk to his office, I give myself a pep talk that thankfully gets me composed before I reach his door.

I knock on the door before opening it and stepping in.

"Sir, you called for me," I say before I look at him to see him not on his seat but half sitting at the front of the table with a stern look on his face and documents in his hand as he keeps his gaze on his phone.

When he finally looks up at me, he does the same swoop with his eyes that troubles my insides, and his eyes soften and gleam as they take in my turquoise blue shirt that is neatly tucked into my ankle-length black pants that does an excellent job in bringing out my shape.

An outfit I had worn without him in mind.

"Miss Field, I had stood on this very spot since I got this documents, waiting for you to step into the office so that I could give them to you to work on them," he says and pauses, taking in my reaction, which I'm sure portrays how guilty I feel.

"I mean I've been standing here for two hours, Miss Field, waiting for you," he continues as he drops his voice low and stares at me directly.

Inappropriately, my body warms up under his gaze, interpreting what he just said in a rather unprofessional way.

"I'm sorry, I kept you waiting sir, I had no idea you had been expecting me," I say to him, and he narrows his eyes and stands up straight, and walks towards me with the documents in his hand.

"Correct me if I'm wrong, but you show up at my office every morning, or am I wrong?" he asks me as he circles me closely, and it makes it hard not to catch a whiff of his cologne which I subtly inhale.

"No sir," I reply to him, feeling trapped both mentally and physically as his scent evades my senses.

"Then what happened today? Could it be that you were avoiding me because of yesterday's incident?" He asks me, standing right in front of me as he looks down at me with his grey eyes boring into mine.

To this, I keep quiet, and his eyes leave mine and go down to my lips as if remembering what happened yesterday, then back to my eyes, and my heartbeat picks up speed.

He lifts his hand and pushes a stray lock of hair behind my ear, gently rubbing my cheeks in the process.

And just like that, the subdued sexual tension sizzles in the air just like yesterday, as I stare at his eyes, captivated by the desiring look in his eyes, and he lowers his head for a kiss very slowly and just as his lips touch mine lightly, I immediately take a quick step back, completely flushed and breathing hard as I look at him shocked at what almost happened again.

"Fuck," he says in barely a whisper as he stands straight, but I hear it.

He puts distance between us, looking at everything but me.

"The… documents," I manage to stutter, and he stretches them to my reach.

I quickly take them from his hands, and, not saying another word, I walk out of his office hurriedly, not stopping until I am safely behind the shut door of my office.

Days pass with similar incidents occurring in different ways, one at the car park, in the elevator, and another just outside the building, times we get dangerously close to giving in to our pure wanton desire.

One thing is clear though, the more we see each other, the more difficult it becomes to keep our hands to ourselves.

6

ISSUES ARISE

NICK'S POV

"I'm telling you that my packaged phones got mixed up with clothes delivery. This is not something I take lightly, Mr. Cross. My customers are not very patient people and they dislike inadequacy," Mr. Sheldon, the owner of Miles Company, complains.

"I will sort it out Mr. Sheldon. I promise this sort of thing will not happen again," I say to him with a calm voice.

"It better not, Mr. Cross, as you know I am a man of principles and one of those principles is not to condone mistakes detrimental to my business," he says, and I nod in agreement.

"I can very well relate Mr. Sheldon, this will not happen again, you have my word," I say to him, trying to appease him.

"The only reason I'm still talking to you nicely about this is because I and your late father go way back. Fix this," He says sternly.

"I understand. I apologize for the inconvenience," I say to him, and he hangs up the call.

I let out a sigh and put my phone down.

This is exactly why I dislike and do not tolerate errors; they always come back to blow up in my face, and needless to say, that is detrimental to the company's reputation.

I look at my wristwatch and check my time to see that it is almost six o'clock, ten minutes to six to be précised, and I sigh again.

Knowing Mr. Sheldon, he would need answers by tomorrow, and no longer than that, so this automatically implies that I will be working throughout the night, trying to find out where exactly the fault came from.

I stand up from the chair and walk out of the office with getting food in mind; if I'm going to be choked up with work for the rest of the night, I would do it while stuffing myself with food.

I stop walking when I see Katrina already prepared to leave and heading towards my direction.

Once she reaches me, she takes in my appearance, and a confused look comes to her face.

"It's already past six, sir, and you don't look ready to leave yet," she asks me, and I shrug.

"That's because I'm not leaving now, or anytime soon for that matter," I say with a cool and unaffected tone.

She gives me a suspicious look as she eyes me again, trying to read off any suspicious vibe.

"Did something happen?" She asks me curiously.

"Nothing much, just major issues to fix and afterwards people to fire," I say casually to her as we still stand in the hallway conversing as others pass, greeting goodnight and exiting the building.

"Your casual tone doesn't hide the fact that this issue seems important, sir. Is there any way I can help?" She asks me with a serious tone and looks, and I smirk at how adorable she looks when she tries to appear serious.

It's the determined and strict look in her eyes right now that is very intimidating to some; that makes her one of my best employees because, with this look, she gets results fast.

"I wouldn't want to bother you, Miss Field," I say dismissively, not intending to keep her stuck in the office with me for hours.

She stares at me quietly for a while, and then the stubborn crease of eyebrow that I see often when she doesn't get what she wants appears on her face.

"You seemed to be on your way out, sir. I'll be waiting for you in your office, I'm sure I can be of help in some way," she says to me, and she begins walking towards my office, not waiting for a response.

For a moment, I think about stopping her and insisting she goes home, but then again, running through every detail and pointing out where the fault came from would be much faster with her present.

Deciding that she can stay and help, I go down to the last floor and exit the building, walking across the road to the number one burger restaurant in town.

Once I get there, I buy two hamburgers, two cheeseburgers, a whole lot of French fries, and two milkshakes.

I walk back into the building, feeling fully prepared to begin work, and I see the place almost empty.

I head up to the elevator, glad that she decided to stay back and help, considering telling a number of times I've stayed late alone, it would be nice to have company this time.

I get into the office to find her sitting down and scrolling through her phone, but she perks up and drops the phone, giving me a surprised look when she sees the burger bags in my hand.

"What?" I ask her with a quirked eyebrow and a flat tone.

"I didn't peg you to be the kind of boss who works and eats at the same time," She says to me clearly amused.

"Well, I am," I say, glaring at her playfully, and she chuckles.

"And I got you some too but if you are not the type to work and eat then I'm keeping all for myself," I say to her, keeping my glare with a straight face, and she laughs at my expression.

"Of course, there's no way I'll let you eat all that alone, you might not fit in your suit," She says, still laughing, a sound which is like a soft melody to my ears.

"You'd be surprised at how much my body can take in," I say to her with a grin as I take a sit beside her, turning my laptop to face me.

"Let's get to work," I say, looking at her, and she nods as she takes out the milkshake from the bag and hands one to me.

"What exactly is the problem?" She asks me, and I explain in detail the major issue we have at hand and the urgency of the situation.

"I didn't spot any error when I had gone through the details of the entire procedure," she says to me, bringing out her laptop from her bag and placing it on the table.

"Neither did I," I admit. "I'm still confused about where the problem came from," I say to her.

"Let me make some calls and find it out," She says as she begins dialing numbers.

"Do that while I'll check with the transport agency and also the receiving wholesale company," I say as I get right to it.

We work for hours, making calls, sending and receiving emails, checking and rechecking facts, and sending and receiving text messages, all to find out the problem.

And this involves a lot of sighs and groans, string of curses, enduring the angry tones of clients over the phone, gulping down burgers and fries, making extra coffee for more working fuel, more sighs and curses, stretching and adjusting our sitting position more than necessary, ignoring the overwhelming urge to fling our phones to the ground out of frustration.

Finally, after going through the hail storm, we spotted the issue and narrowed it down to the logistics of the shipment.

So basically, my entire problem was caused by incompetent personnel in the logistics department; he or she made a mistake and covered it up expertly well, and both Katrina and I did not notice when we checked.

Though, it looks like the mistake was made more out of ignorance than purposefulness.

Now, we have to figure out how to correct this error without greatly affecting the shipment's accounts so that the corrections can be sent to the wholesale company.

With that, the corrections can be effected, and the two goods differentiated so that the textiles can be reshipped to their original location.

It takes us another hour to finalize everything, thirty minutes to figure out the alterations to be made, and an extra thirty minutes explaining to the different required sectors why the changes were made and how they should be affected.

"Finally, fuck! I'm beat," Katrina says with a sigh as she checks the time.

"Jeez, it's eleven o'clock," she says, looking between me and her wristwatch surprised.

"At least we've accomplished our task, there are days I would stay this late and end up not achieving what I set out to," I say to her, stretching my joints before standing up.

"I guess you are right," she says as she puts her laptop back in her bag and stands up prepared to leave.

"Well, have a good night sir," she says to me with a smile which I return.

"I really appreciate your help today," I say as I step closer to her with gratitude prominent on my features.

"It's fine, besides, you fed me well," She says with light humor, and I grin at her statement.

"I'm really grateful Kat, I couldn't have done this without you," I say to her, calling her a nickname that I didn't realize I used until it was already out of my mouth.

If she heard it, she chose to ignore it.

"Of course you would have," she says.

"I mean it," I start saying as I take her hand in mine, "I couldn't have done this without you, it probably would have taken me forever to figure it out on my own," I drop my voice to low octave and stare deep into her eyes.

She doesn't reply but rather unexpectedly gets on her tiptoes and gives me a light, quick peck.

Surprised by the sudden kiss, I freeze up for a moment.

"I'm sorry sir," she says, looking embarrassed as she immediately removes her hand from mine and turns to walk away in haste.

But before she takes two steps, I grab her hand again, stopping her.

Closing the gap between us, I dip my head low and capture her lips in a hot searing kiss, and not three seconds later, she returns the kiss with the same fervor, throwing her hand around my neck and keeping me in place, as she molds her lips with mine.

I grab her waist and pull her closer to myself as I nibble her lips seeking entrance, which she willingly grants as I use my tongue to explore her mouth while both our tongues dance sensually together.

I tilt her head and deepen the kiss, and I feel her cling to me with weak knees as she moans into the kiss.

"I just knew you'd be in here," Christian says, making our kiss end abruptly, and she immediately distances herself from me.

"Whoa!" he says in surprise with a huge grin on his face, and I run my hand through my hair.

"Goodnight," Katrina says quietly with a flushed face, looking embarrassed at being caught in the act.

I simply nod in response as she walks away hurriedly.

"What do you want, Christian?" I ask him, glaring, once I see that Katrina is gone.

"Well hello to you too brother, I see you were enjoying your night and didn't need interruptions," he says with a smirk, teasingly, with an amused glint in his eyes.

I maintain my glare, silently telling him I'm in no mood for jokes.

"Well I went over to your house and you were not there. Knowing you, I figured you would be here," he says finally, and I look at him suspiciously.

"What went wrong this time?" I ask him because it's strange that he would go to the extent of going to my house to look for me and then go further by coming here.

"We need to talk," He says with a sigh as he sits down, and I know it's something very important.

7

NICK'S WARNING

KATRINA'S POV

I ran out of the building, embarrassed by what happened.

To think his brother walked in on us as we were making out.

Fuck! We actually made out.

I get into my car and slam the door shut harder than necessary because of the impact of the thought.

I place my head on the steering wheel, try to calm my nerves and wait for my breathing to normalize.

At this point, I don't know what exactly was making me breathe erratically. Is it the effect of the race? I ran out of the building, or is it the embarrassment I felt when I saw the smug look on Christian's face when he saw both of us kissing, or is it the mind-blowing kiss itself?

Not wanting to spend more time outside alone and not in the

comfort and safety of my home, I lift my head from the steering wheel and start up the car engine, pulling out of the car park and heading home with a warm bath in mind.

Not surprisingly, I don't get home before my thoughts rush back into my mind, reminding me that I had kissed my boss in his office.

And not just any boss, the same one that had a relationship with his past secretary, the same one that gave me a promotion on my first day without any form of interview to judge if I was suitable for the position, but considering my capability based on my appearance.

But then again, he is the same boss who has been nothing but respectful to me, not once trying to do anything to make me uncomfortable and not once invading my personal space.

Well, until recently, when I gave him silent permission to invade that space, and just like everything he does, he did it so skillfully well that the space doesn't feel so personal anymore.

He is just like that hot visitor that you give a spare room on the first visit, without a request, deciding to be roommates with him, and maybe more.

He stomped in and took his place, a place I didn't realize was even available until he filled it, and now I feel crowded in a deliciously overwhelming way, and I want more.

This time, the kiss was even better than the first; it seemed more profound and intimate, like a sense of familiarity between us.

If there was restraint and caution in the last kiss, then this one was total surrender and acceptance.

The passion he expressed through a single kiss makes me wonder what it would fill like if we had gone beyond that, how it would have felt to have him take me right there in his office.

I push the sinful thought that has already started becoming vivid and more detailed out of my mind, and I step down from my car as I reach my house.

I unlock my door and step inside, thankful to be back in the warmth of a house and able to remove the heavy clothing on my body.

I walk into my room, stripped completely, and make a beeline for the shower.

After having a good and warm bath, I put on light clothes and fall right into my bed, and unlike other nights, I fall asleep immediately due to the extra stress and mind-blowing sensation I got today.

The next day, I walked into Torrent's company, and just like other days, since winter started, it's buzzing with staff working double time.

I head towards the elevator as usual, but unlike other days, I feel extra excited to see Nick today.

Somewhere between my dreams of him and my conscious state at night, I had agreed that ignoring my insane attraction towards him would be fruitless.

I decided that a little sexual activity was just what I needed, and since he has proven to be way more than the little I expected him to be, starting something real with him would not hurt because there is also no denying that along the line, I had developed more than just sexual feelings for him.

Feelings shocked me upon realization, feelings that I had put a solid lock on. Now, I've decided that considering what I've been through in my past relationship, there is no way I would develop feelings for another jerk.

Or so I believe.

So with this motivation, and also the very aggressive encouragement I got from my best friend at three in the morning, who drunk dialed me and somehow made me tell her everything that was making me go in and out of sleep, that I'm sure she doesn't remember now.

I accept my feelings rather than ignore them and see where it leads even though my job is in potential danger.

I reach the hallway leading to my office and walk speedily towards it, eager to drop my bag and put off the winter accessories so I can finally see Nick.

When I reach my office, I open my door to a shocking sight.

There's another lady in my office, sitting on my chair with her hands on my desk, who suddenly smiles when she sees me.

"Hello, good morning. You must be Miss Katrina Field. I'm Carrie Stewards," she says with an overly chirpy voice that stings a little as she walks towards me and stretches her hand out for a handshake.

"Miss Stewards, what exactly is going on here?" I ask her as I take the handshake, not bothering to keep a pleasant tone.

"Actually, it's Mrs. Stewards, I'm married," she says with a bright smile as she shows me her ring.

I ensure to school my features and withhold my tongue at how irrelevant what she just said is right now as I plaster a smile on my face.

"Congratulations," I say simply with a stiff tone, hinting that I need answers as to why the hell she is in my office.

She seems to get the hint and straightens up.

"Mr. Cross instructed that we switch offices, he said that I should inform you that all matters that would need physical interaction with him should be done through me," she says to me, and I stare at her, shocked.

"I don't understand, I got demoted from the secretarial position?" I ask her, completely surprised.

"Oh no, you are still the secretary, I'm the head of the logistics department, so let's just say he decided to keep a closer eye on me because of a slip up, which I'm not proud of," She says and continues.

"All we did was switch offices, not position. You can say that I'm like an intermediary between you and him for the main time. He said it's not permanent but indefinite," She finishes still with a very chirpy and friendly voice, and I feel absolutely annoyed.

"Okay, thank you, Mrs. Stewards," I say to her simply, trying so hard to keep my voice passive and avoid glaring at her.

"You are very welcome. I could show you to your new office, it's just down the hall," she offers with a bright smile.

"I'll find it myself, thank you," I say, trying to sound polite but rather strained.

I walk out of the office without waiting for a reply, shutting the door harder than necessary, and march straight to Nick's office.

What the heck is this about?

He kissed me yesterday and decided I was no longer worthy of seeing him physically.

I get to his office, and just as I am about to knock, the door opens, and Mr. Grant, a fellow staff walks out.

We exchange greetings before I enter his office without

knocking.

"What the hell is going on?" I ask him in an angry tone, not bothering to greet him.

"Tone, Miss Field," He says with a passive voice, not looking up, but I can swear I saw him flinch slightly when he heard my voice.

"Good morning to you, Miss Field. I'm sure you've heard of the changes I made," he says, finally looking at me with a poker face.

I glare at him for five good seconds before I reply to him, and he gives me the pleasure of showing discomfort during those seconds.

"You moved me to another office further away from yours and gave strict instructions that I am not to see you physically, all because of a kiss," I state rather than ask with my voice sounding hurt rather than angry, much to my dislike.

To this, he stands up from his chair and turns around the table to meet me, though ensuring to keep the distance between us.

"Two kisses, Katrina. Not one. It is clear that we can't seem to keep our hands off each other when we are alone. I don't want such a thing reaching the eyes or ears of another staff, it's highly unprofessional, so I had to put an end to it," He says, stating the plain fact.

"So the best way you could think of remedy the situation is to ensure that we don't see eye to eye," I look at him in disbelief, almost with a mocking glare.

"It seems like a good idea, besides, the other option would be to fire you, but that would be unmerited and also I can't bring myself to do that," He says, keeping his voice gentle and soothing, and I glare even harder at him.

"So what, we are just to go on about our days and act like nothing ever happened, and that this tension in the air is non-existent?" I ask him as I start walking closer to him but stop when he takes a step back, I feel hurt by his withdrawal, but I mask it behind my annoyance.

"Damn, Kat! I'm trying to save your job here. I can't have anyone find out about this thing between us or I'll be forced to fire you," He says to me, and I feel my hurt become more prominent.

"Why?" I ask him with a very quiet voice.

"Why what?" he asks.

"Why do you have to fire me if they find out?" I ask him.

"Because it's unprofessional and inappropriate. I would not condone or tolerate such a thing going on between other staffs and disrupting the flow of work," He says to me, and I nod slowly, not in acceptance but in surrender.

"Okay, I'll go to my office now," I say to him, with hurt clearly projected through my voice.

I turn to leave, not waiting for any other heart-lashing word from him.

"Kat," he calls out as I reach the door, and I freeze up at the use of my nickname again.

"This is not easy for me either. You don't know how much I want you and wish things were different," he says to me in a passionate tone.

"You shouldn't say things like that to me when you want me to leave, Mr. Cross," I say to him, looking at him dead in the eyes, and I open the door and walk out.

I walk through the hallway as I search for my office, slowly scanning my eyes over each name tag.

I finally find it, at the farthest side from his own; I sigh and open the door.

Getting inside, I take off my coat and slump right into a chair, exhausted for the day, even though I haven't started working yet.

I lean my head back on the headrest and think of how ridiculous this entire thing is. Just when I had decided to put aside those walls of caution, I got shipped away from him.

At least, I'm sure I'm not the only one affected by this.

With this thought, I stand up and pour coffee into a cup, preparing it to my taste, determined to be the less miserable one amongst both of us.

Besides, compared to the scars on my heart that I got from my deranged ex, this hurt should be a piece of cake.

With this determination, I dove right into work, completely pushing Nick out of my mind.

8

SECRET MEETINGS

I didn't think meeting her and telling her what I had decided on would be that hard; when she came in spitting out hot coal from her tongue, I was sort of relieved.

Relieved that at least she was just angry at me because anger is an emotion that can be managed without causing much damage in our situation.

But then, when I looked up and saw the expression on her face and the look in her eyes, I knew it wasn't going to be easy talking to her.

She wore the look of anger to mask her hurt, and I hate that I was able to see through it because I'm sure I'll be better off not knowing that under that angry façade, she was truly hurt.

Another overwhelming thing was the hurtful tug I felt in my heart as she shut the door to my office.

I sat on a spot and stared at the door for good twenty minutes with my mind swirling, thinking of different ways to make the situation better.

If only it was under different circumstances, then I wouldn't have had to let her go and endure the ache and painful drums my heart kept beating non-stop.

I had sat there and only stood up when I got a call that brought me out of my daze. Currently, I'm still trying to figure out who the black sheep in my board of directors is.

The night Christian had come here, he gave me very disturbing news.

He told me that he saw a letter at the front of his door from an unknown sender that stated broadly-discussed reasons why he should use the power of his position to remove me from my position as the company's manager.

The most disturbing reason the letter stated is that once his three years as CEO elapsed, and I took over the CEO position, I would throw him to the curb.

Also that I will most likely leave him out of everything that concerns the company, cutting him off completely because I see him as a liability.

In an addition to that right now would be the right time to frame me for doing something wrong and then bring the matter up with the board, whom the sender promised would be in total and complete support of him to remove me from my position and completely take away all rights I have over the company.

The guts they have to even attempt this is because my father clearly stated that if I were to get involved in something unethical and illegal, then I should be stripped of all my rights, and the company should be left in the hands of his best friend, who is our major suspect.

Right now, we just need to gather enough evidence against him to forcefully take him out of the board of directors.

This shouldn't be difficult if he really is the one behind this, but he is my late father's best friend.

Right now, I'm just thankful that Christian trusts me enough not to believe such a ploy and not follow through with it because if there is anyone who can frame me successfully, it would be him.

At least he knows that there is no way in hell I will leave him out of the company's earnings completely.

It's just left with three months for him to hand over the position to me, and that's why such things are sprouting up to completely take the company from our hands.

Needless to say that their efforts are futile. Right now, the investigation is being carried out, and we will soon have results.

This sort of thing arising doesn't shock me in the slightest; coups and ploys always arise within the board of directors, this isn't the first time, but I will ensure that it is the last time it is this drastic.

Knowing that those old men's strategies always lack proper analysis to go over each gap or missed out weakness in their plan, it shouldn't take much time to figure the culprit out.

I'll ensure that it's done and the entire matter is resolved before Christmas.

It's now been three days since I set my eyes on Katrina, three extremely lonely days.

I had tried so hard to drown all thoughts of her out and focus solely on work, but that didn't work out, as little things made my thoughts keep going back to her.

Ever since Christian settled my suspicion about her hitting on him by telling me that she had rejected his offer to take her on a date and completely turned him down when he asked, I didn't have any other solid reason to avoid my attraction towards her.

Each time Mrs. Stewards would walk into the room with a message from Katrina, it would further prove how dumb as fuck my plan to stay away from her was because, in this case, with each message I received from her, the more my longing to see her increased.

At least with her here, I wouldn't be this restless and unable to focus on work because my heart just can't seem to come to terms with the fact that it's supposed to be playing the part of letting go.

I didn't even know when my heart became a factor to consider, but as the days went by and I didn't see that smiling face of hers, that annoyed scowl on her face, those smooth and sexy strides when she walked away from me, swaying her hips sensually, I knew that I was hooked.

As each day passed, I knew just how much, somewhere between the sensual kisses and the sexual lust, I had developed real feelings for her that this distance was becoming bothersome to my mental health.

I check my time and see that it is two minutes past the closing time; I stand up, pack my things and leave the office hurriedly, in the hope of at least seeing her today before I leave.

I walk down the hallway, past the elevator, and towards her office to see her coming right towards me with a surprised look on her face.

"Mr. Cross," She greets as she looks at me with a lifted

eyebrow, and I smile, not being able to help myself; I had missed her deeply.

"Miss Field," I say with a smile still gracing my features, and I see her eyes soften as she takes in the crystal clear look of happiness on my face and smiles lightly too.

We stand in the hallway looking like two reunited lovers, completely in our own zone with grateful smiles on our faces and an intense look in our eyes, completely ignoring the strange stares we get from others as they rush out of the building.

I take in her appearance, and a warm feeling moves through my body, causing me to breathe out softly. I had expected this exact look, thicker coats, thicker gloves and an additional scarf.

It is the fifteenth day of December, and the cold is very noticeable. You can now find everyone putting on winter clothes, unlike her, who started wearing hers on the second day when the cold had barely begun.

My eyes land on the file in her hand and stay there before looking at her with a questioning look.

"I was coming to give it to you at your office since Mrs. Stewards had already called it a day," She says with a quiet voice, and I can tell she is lying about her reason, besides I had just seen Mrs. Stewards leave her office as I walked here, surely she wouldn't have minded giving it to me.

I smirk at her obvious lie, and my heart softens yet again that she had attempted to see me today as well.

I walk closer to her without any atom of reasoning, as if drawn, and place a light kiss on her lips, which she leans into, but I shorten the kiss, conscious of where we are. The soft feel remained, and I could feel my heart working well again.

"I missed you," I say to her, and her smile brightens.

"Same," she says.

"How about I take you on a date tomorrow, after work," I say to her, instantly coming up with the idea, and she looks at me with her eyes wide in surprise.

"Really?" She asks me, and I nod, serious about my request.

"Yes," she says simply with a huge smile on her face, and she gives me another quick kiss.

"Okay then, immediately after work, we'll meet at the car park and then I'll drive us," I say to her, gently running my hand down her cheek in an affectionate manner.

She nods and smiles in response as she leans into my touch.

***

The next day was slower than usual, but the entire day passed in a blur, as all I could focus on was the date afterward.

Before long, we are both driving in my car on our way to The Ritz Carlton, with huge grins on our faces.

We both make small talk as we drive there as we both ease out the office tension.

Once we reach our destination and park the vehicle, I step down and turn to open the door for her, offering my hand.

"Did I tell you how beautiful you look today?" I say to her as she gets down, and she smirks.

"If you think I'm beautiful now, wait till you see me all dolled up after a relaxed day, and not having to rush preparations after a hectic day at work," She says in a calm tone as we walk into the restaurant.

"I would love to see you that way, how about another date

tomorrow, and this time, we could spend the entire day together?" I say to her and see her expression turn into a surprised one.

"How about we see how this date goes and then I decide if you even have a chance of taking me on another date?" She says with a teasing smirk.

"Katrina, I never fail to sweep my dates off their feet," I say to her with a confident smirk.

"We shall see Nickolas," she says, looking amused by my confidence.

Once we are seated, we both order from the Prix Fixe Menu, she gets the Lobster bisque, while I have the Wagyu beef.

I had booked a private seat, still taking extra precautions that we don't get seen by anybody we know.

We spend the entire night eating, laughing, and getting to know each other better. But even with this bliss, we still keep in mind that our affair needs to remain private, and as much as it is not a comfortable situation for both of us, it's the only one we can afford right now.

Given my strict office policy and the fact that I cannot afford to be caught doing anything unprofessional right now with the heat from the board of directors, we just have to stick to stealing secret kisses at work and have hidden dates afterward.

I am most grateful that she accepted these conditions when I explained it to her, though not giving her full details about the issue at hand.

After our dinner, I drive her home, and after getting her acceptance for the date tomorrow, and also not failing to kiss her goodnight, I drive back home feeling fulfilled and happy.

Feelings I have not had in a long time.

I get back home and take a shower, exhausted for the day but excited for the next day. I start making plans for our next secret meeting as I get ready for bed.

I must say, as much as it should feel wrong that I am going against my laid down principles of not fraternizing with my employee, it feels so right being with her.

I fall asleep midst thinking of her, and I wake to the exciting knowledge that I get to spend my whole Sunday with her and, hopefully, the early hours of Monday before we get back to hiding around and pretending that nothing is going on between us.

Having a quick bath and dressing in plain Jeans and a polo shirt, I leave the house and head to her place, determined to make the best of these hours I get to spend with her.

9

STEAMY MOMENTS

I wake up to the sound of my alarm clock, which I had forgotten to turn off yesterday.

Since the workload has become double what it used to be ever since winter started, all staff now have to work for six days a week, having only Sunday as a resting day.

So I had completely forgotten to shut off the damn thing before sleeping yesterday, with today being Sunday.

I get off my bed feeling very excited and in a very good mood as my mind goes over everything that happened yesterday when me and Nickolas went out.

He had been amazing, showering me with compliments, not too much to make the entire thing cliché but just right to make me feel like the prettiest lady in the room.

And he didn't end the date with just dinner at one of the best hotels in Chicago but also took me to the rooftop lounge where we had the most amazing view of Lake Michigan.

What marveled me most was the complete change of personality that he displayed. He suddenly turned from a strict man with limited words to a very jovial man full of laughter, fun, and jokes.

I cannot count how many times he made me laugh yesterday or how many new facial expressions of his that I got to see as he tried to dramatize some of the jokes he told.

Some ended up making no sense, but they still cracked me up nonetheless.

He was a perfect gentleman yesterday, from the time he opened the door for me before we got into the hotel to the time he dropped me off at home and walked me to my door, not doing any other thing but giving me a simple kiss.

I knew very well that with just a little effort from him, things would have taken a different turn, but he was so careful not to cross that limit on our first date, and this completely erased my opinion of him as a pervert.

No pervert would be that controlled; I have had first-hand experience of lack of control, so I can testify that Nickolas is everything but that.

I walk into the bathroom and take a quick bath, eager to get prepared before he shows up to pick me up for our date.

I couldn't say no to him when he asked me the second time if I would let him take me out today; every fiber of my being screamed yes within me, but I managed to rein my excitement and give him a simple moderate toned yes.

I walk out of the bathroom and search my wardrobe for something simple to put on as he had instructed, and I settle with a simple Jean trousers and a blue flower patterned top.

I put it on and focus on applying light make-up, a little powder, eyeliner, and gloss is enough to make me look pretty good to go out with him.

Just as I'm done perfecting my makeup, I hear the doorbell ring, and I hurry to the front door, fully aware that he is the one.

"Good morning, beautiful," he says to me with a cheery voice as he points a bouquet of flowers at me and I smile broadly at the sight.

"Good morning," I reply as I take the flowers from him and smell it, inhaling its lovely scent.

"Ready?" he asks me, and I nod before I walk inside to put the lilies in a vase and pick up my purse.

"Let's go," I say as I walk back out and lock my door.

"Before that," he says and bends down and takes my lips in a simple but very sensual kiss and feels a familiar warmth within as I lean into the kiss; his tongue swipes down my lips, and just as I am about to open up-

"Mm, now let's go," He says as he breaks the kiss with a smirk on his face, and I get down from my high zone and follow him to his car.

Tease.

I would have never thought I would be going on a date with my boss, or even going on a date at all, but here I am, letting him shower me with time and attention as he drives me off to our second date, which I must say feels amazing already.

"So, where are we going to?" I ask him as he drives with his eyes on the road.

"It's a surprise," he says to me with a sly smile on his face, with his eyes still focused on the road.

"The last time someone said that to me, I got chained up and whipped for fun," I say to him in humor without thinking.

"What?" He asks, completely surprised as he stares at me.

It's only when I see the surprised look in his eyes that color drains from my face as I realize what I just said in the form of a joke to him.

"What did you say, Kat?" he asks me again, this time more serious as he takes in my expression.

I remain quiet for a while, still thinking up an excuse to give him.

"It was a joke," I say, not being able to think of any other creative thing to say, and the look on his face tells me he doesn't buy it.

"That's obviously a lie Kat," he says, but I remain quiet, wondering how I had let something that sensitive slip out.

"Shit, are you crying? Kat, I will pull this car over if you don't tell me the meaning of what you just said now and don't lie to me," He says with his voice raised slightly and extremely serious; care etched all over his features.

I don't realize that I am crying until I feel tears roll down my cheeks, and I hear myself sob.

"Pull over," I say to him with my voice barely above a whisper, but he hears and complies immediately.

Once he pulls over to a side, he turns and faces me, giving me his full attention.

"I don't know how to answer your question Nick, I don't even know how that slipped out," I say to him between sobs, completely confused about how to start telling him that I was sexually abused by a man I loved.

"Hey, it's alright, I don't want you to feel pressured about this, you don't have to tell me right now," He says to me in concern after observing me for a while as he wipes the tears off my cheek and leans in and peppers kiss all over my face.

I stay quiet for a while, trying to contain my tears and get myself together, wondering how today went from extremely happy to teary and sad.

"Would you also understand if I tell you that I don't really feel like going out anymore," I ask him, and I hold my breath and shut my eyes tightly, waiting for his answer?

"Honestly, I don't think where I had planned for us to go would still be a good idea today, so it's fine," he says. I release the breath I hold, and a smile comes to my face as I see the tender look in his eyes.

Without thinking, I lean closer and capture his lips in a kiss, molding my lips into his and moving them slowly as he lets me lead the kiss. His eyes are still looking at me in surprise till they soften almost naturally.

He parts his lips for me and lets me deepen the kiss as our tongues mold together, he groans a bit and I shudder, tingles moving through my body.

I cross over to the driver seat, adjusting my position until I am straddling him, and he places his hand on my hips, pulling me close to him so that I can feel his erection through his coat. His breath quickens as his hands squeeze on my hips, causing me to grind into him more fervently.

"Fuck Kat. We have to stop," he says to me between short breaths as I keep kissing him down his neck, biting and nibbling slowly and he lets out a groan in response. My mind is clouded and lost in the world of Nick.

"Kat, you really need to stop now," he says to me as he pulls me away from him gently and I stare at him confused.

"I can't take you in my car beautiful, it's not right," he continues, seeing the confused look on my face, and I stare at him for a while, conflicted with emotions.

Part of me appreciates what a responsible fellow he is, and the other part dislikes the fact that he is actually this responsible.

With a sigh, I get off him and move back to my seat, settling in, putting on my seatbelt, and facing the window, not looking at him. My breaths are still soft, and I have no plans of calming down either.

"Are you okay?" he asks with concern, and as much as I want to smile at how caring he is, my needy and aching body wants him now.

"Is your house close by?" I ask him with a quiet voice as I look at him, and he seems to get the hint as he smirks and starts the car engine, putting his feet on the accelerator.

I take deep breaths to calm myself down and avoid jumping him as he is driving. I take notice of trees and roads, counting numbers like a held-down puppy.

It doesn't take long, and we are at his house, which happens to be a mansion, not that I am completely surprised, considering he is the manager and soon will be the CEO of a flourishing exporting company.

He drives in and parks his car in his massive garage filled with different car models.

"When you said you have a thing for cars, I didn't know it was this serious." I say in awe as I step down from the car and look at the assorted expensive array of cars.

"Let's just say when I'm passionate about something, I tend to take it to the extreme," he says, and I turn to see him staring right at me with a smile on his face and an intense look in his eyes, and I feel the fire that started growing cold ignite again as my body warms up under his gaze.

"Let's go in," I say to him, already at the brisk of losing my patience.

He doesn't say another word as he takes my hand and leads me into his home. I don't bother checking out once he shuts the front door, I pounce on him, kissing him hungrily, and he returns each kiss with the same fervor.

Midst kissing each other, we both take off our coats as we try to maintain physical contact, and then we take off our shoes which thankfully don't require the use of our hands.

Once we are done with the removal of our shoes, we go right back to kissing each other with more hunger, like that brief moment of not being lip locked made us even more starved for each other.

He picks me up and leads me up the stairs, which I barely pay focus to, and lust clouds my mind as I feel his tongue plunge in and out of my mouth in a delicious manner, and I moan at the sensation.

All forms of reasoning leave my mind as I get lost in the pleasure that keeps magnifying as each second passes.

He walks into a room that I assume is him based on the dark

interior, even though it's mid-day, and drops me on the bed gently.

He breaks the kiss, which earns a whine from me, and he takes his shirt off, much to my delight, as I take in his muscled chest, which looks even more sexy than it was in my imagination. Why is it so beautiful?

He doesn't give me much time to admire his physic as he comes back on top of me and kisses me deeply on my lips before moving down slowly to earlobe, which he sucks lightly, earning a throaty moan from me.

His hand goes under my top, and he runs his finger over the hem of my bra as I arc my back slightly, giving him the chance to unhook it.

Once he unhooks it, he brings his hands back to the front and palms my breast, giving it a light squeeze as he runs his thumb over my nipple, making me arc into his hand, needing more pressure which he doesn't hesitate to apply.

Still laying kisses on my neck, he takes his hand out of the top to the edge and starts to take it up, seeming tired of it being an obstruction, and I let him do it, eager to be rid of my clothes.

He takes the top off and then the bra, and my medium-sized boobs spill free on full display before his hungry gaze.

"Beautiful," he whispers as he bends and latches his lips onto a nipple as he sucks, flicks, and nibbles it like it is the most delicious treat he has ever had.

He moves his lips to the next one and renders the same sensual onslaught to it as his hand goes over the first one and does the same thing, and I become a moaning mess underneath him.

"Fuck, Nick, I need more," I say to him, moaning loudly, and with incredible skill and speed, he ensures that we are both naked.

He takes his time to offer me intense pleasure, and I find myself having multiple orgasms as I scream his name in ecstasy multiple times.

Once we are both sated of our hunger, we lay on the bed, our bodies tangled together in peaceful silence.

I simply enjoy the feeling of just being in his arms as my heart swells with emotions.

At this point, I know that there is no denying the fact that I have fallen hopelessly and helplessly in love with this man that managed to skillfully spin his web around my senses and masterfully make me let go of all my inhibitions.

10

CONFLICT

NICK'S POV

"**I** believe it is inappropriate of you to have an affair with your secretary Mr. Cross. It is against our ethics, as it clearly states in the regulations that any form of relationship between staff that would bring about hindrance to the workflow in the company leads to immediate sack of the parties involved, Mr. Saltzman says to me with a stern voice.

I'm currently in a board meeting with every single board member in attendance, and right now, Mr. Saltzman, my late father's best friend and my major suspect of the mysterious letter Christian received, reveals himself as the culprit he truly is.

To think he used my relationship with Katrina as leverage to back up his despicable agenda.

I have no idea how he found out about both of us, but for him to use her as the only backing he has, means that he is desperate and grasping for all the straws he can find.

I look around at the table and see all eyes on me, waiting for a response, but all I can think of right now, and all that has been on my mind since yesterday, is the detailed explanation Katrina had given me about her past relationship and everything she had gone through.

It's been two days since we had sex, and she finally opened up to me yesterday night after another passionate round of pleasure.

She told me how she had been in a relationship for two years, and within those two years, she had been a victim of sexual assault and couldn't say or do anything about it.

She told me that it all started out as a little bit of adventure when she and her ex-boyfriend had both sought to spice up their relationship and broaden their sexual horizon.

She said it had all been fine until he introduced BDSM into their sexual life; at first, she said she didn't really have much of a problem with it because he asked for her consent on everything he did to her and what she did not support, he would completely rule it out.

But she said it changed slowly as time went on; he got more excited about the new ideas he found out, and he kept bringing up movies and pictures of the various ideas he wanted them to try, and when she had kicked against some, he paid no mind to her and still went ahead with it.

He choked her, whipped her, and cut her deeply with a knife severally until she would pass out of excessive bleeding, all for his pleasure.

She said that every time he did that, for the next week, he would dedicate his entire time to making her forgive him, and when she did, he would go right back to his former ways, but each time developing more creative ways to hurt her and use her body for his pleasure.

She told me all these things, and not a single tear rolled down her face, as she kept an impassive look, saying it like it is a normal experience that every woman has, sounding like the horror she went through at the hands of the monster that abused her is as easy as normal as having a monthly cycle.

I felt so enraged when she told me all these things, and till now, I have an intense urge to find that bastard and make him pay for what he did to her.

Find him and hurt him terribly for scarring that beautiful woman for life, for making her stay depressed and waste two good years of her life.

One thing I have gotten from her story and her experiences is that she is the exact opposite of the feeble appearance she portrays, that inside that weak coverage, there is a strong woman who has learned to become a survivor and overcome all the challenges in life throws at her, chase away all her demons and powerfully push forward, staying optimistic but extremely careful about what life has to offer.

I envy her strength as I know that most people in her shoes would not open up to any man sexually or emotionally in such a short period of time as she did.

"Nick, what do you have to say for yourself?" Patrick, another member of the board, says to me, bringing me out of my thoughts.

I can feel the tension in the room as everyone stares at me, waiting for me to seal my faith, some hoping that I lose while some hoping that I scale through.

"First, I will like to know where exactly such an accusation is coming from?" I ask, still maintaining my passive face as I put my full focus into the meeting, determined to preserve my reputation and also uproot the weed in this garden whilst doing so.

"For the past two days, some of your employees have noticed an unmerited display of favoritism between you and Miss Field and one employee claims to have seen both of you in a very compromising position in your office yesterday," Mr. Saltzman says.

At his last statement, I feel the tension in the room thicken as various accusing eyes focus on me.

I can't help the energetic feeling that sprouts up within me at the magnitude of this issue; it has been a long time since we have had this sort of conflict in the company, the last time was when my father was alive, and Christian had been the one on the hot seat, and the feeling of being completely on top of the situation is thrilling.

"Not that I am trying to prolong this issue, but was that employee specific in her description of the compromising position she found both of us in," I ask with a bored tone, because what I'm doing is actually prolonging this entire thing, but the extra confident look on Mr. Saltzman's face is what is driving me to prolong this.

The thought of the euphoria I will feel when he realizes that he lost this worthless battle before it even began, as his face drains of all its color, is just too fulfilling to pass up.

"That is completely unnecessary Mr. Cross, go ahead and answer the question." Says Mr. Gate, also one of the board members.

I note each person that speaks and keep them in mind.

"In that case, in response to his accusation, I have a tape of every activity that went on in my office for the past two days, if you all will like to watch it," I say to all of them and not wait for their response as I put on the recording, and it displays on the projector screen.

Taking proper precautions and taking into consideration that one way or the other, my relationship with Katrina might likely be found out, I had put a camera in my office, prepared for something like this.

The room falls silent as I display scenes that each employee had walked in and out of my office for the past two days.

The particular one, Katrina and I had been in the office together as another employee walked in, I zoomed in clearly to show our position, just as Mrs. Stewards had walked in, and I stared at the screen with rapt attention, ignoring the glare from Mr. Saltzman directed at me, who can do nothing but watch quietly.

The screen clearly shows Katrina pointing out something on the laptop screen as she stands close to me, and Mrs. Stewards walks in on us.

It also shows that even after she walked in, Katrina had not moved from her position and kept explaining what was wrong with her.

The heavy tension in the room lightens up a bit as smirks and smiles come on to some faces, and some frown as they see the innocence of the situation.

"As true and as vivid as this might be Mr. Cross, somethings do not add up," he says to me, and I smirk, already knowing exactly what he is going to say.

"I'm sure that you are referring to the fact that I had given Miss Field instructions to pass all information that would require physical contact between both of us through Mrs. Steward, am I right?" I say, and the tension in the room thickens again.

"Yes Mr. Cross, care to explain that?" he says, and I try to reign my laughter as his entire attempt to save face becomes humorous to me.

"Well, I gave that instruction as a form of punishment to Mrs. Steward for a huge error she made while working, and at the same time, it was also a form of award to Miss Field for her excellent work as my secretary, I sought to reduce her stress," I say and pause, slowly taking a sip of my water before continuing.

"After one week, I saw that the instruction made our job harder than necessary for us so I took back my instruction and made sure Miss Field informed Mrs. Steward about this, which I am sure she did," I say, and he remains silent and glaring at me.

"In the same vain of bringing open unprofessional and unethical doings, I would like everyone to look at the file I just sent," I say, and everyone opens up the file and gaps fill the room as fear fills Mr. Saltzman's eyes and all eyes turn to him in disbelief.

"To add to this Mr. Saltzman, my private life and whom I choose to have a relationship with is completely up to me. As you quoted the company's regulation, as long as it doesn't affect the workflow within the company your opinion as to what is professional and unprofessional doesn't matter to me, I only went along with this baseless argument to prove clearly that your accusation holds no ground," I say with a very stern voice and just as I imagined, blood drains out of his face as he looks white in fear.

***

"What can I say, he had it coming," I say with a laugh to Christian after the meeting.

"Fuck! It was so badass the way you kept your cool and he kept heating up with each come back you came up with," he says as he places his hand on my shoulder.

"Thanks, it was fun seeing all the defense he thought he put up well crumble right before him," I say with a proud smile on my face.

"I'm just grateful that he is now out of the way, with the evidence of fraud you have on him, there is no way he is getting out of jail in very long time," Christian says.

"Yeah," I say simply, as typically, he had already started walking away before he said his last word, probably off to some club to celebrate.

I sigh at the thought and walk towards my office, grateful that that episode is over.

Mr. Saltzman will be well behind bars in no time.

It didn't take much effort to find out and compile all his fraudulent activities, money laundering being the most significant one of all.

I had made sure to dig up enough evidence to ensure that nothing he does stops him from receiving his punishment.

My mind goes back to Katrina and the fact that she has vehemently refused to tell me the name of the monster who had hurt her, insisting that she has put it all in the past and she doesn't want any reason to have to revisit it.

No matter how many times I had tried to convince her to tell me the name that I would do nothing, even though that was a lie, she refused and made me promise not to look it up, telling me to respect her decision to keep it buried.

As much as it annoys me that I couldn't inflict pain back on the bastard, I understand that she doesn't in no way want to have any form of connection with him, and my getting involved would bring up a kind of connection between both of them again.

Changing my mind about going to my office and eager to see her after so many hours, I walk towards her office.

I knock on the door once I reach it, and her light voice reaches out, telling me to come in.

"How about we ditch work for the rest of the day?" I ask her with a teasing smirk, and she smiles widely in reply.

"I don't think that is a good idea, boss," she says with a smirk as she takes in my appearance.

"How did it go?" she asks curiously.

"As expected," I say simply as I slump on the chair, exhausted and ready to call it a day.

"Are you sure I cannot convince you to stop work for the day?" I ask her, and she chuckles.

"Well someone's really eager." she says teasingly, and I smile as I look at how pretty she is.

My mind goes over the fact that in this short period of time, I have come to care for her deeply that I would go to great lengths just to make her happy.

And then it dawns on me that I have fallen so deeply in love with this woman that, against all odds, I don't want to keep a secret anymore.

11

THE REVEAL

Not in the least bit concerned, Nick had met me and informed me that somehow one of his board members had found out about our relationship, and I had freaked out completely, scared for both of us.

I kept thinking of ways he could have found out because we both ensured to kccp things official as long as we were in the office, and with the way we acted, there was no way anyone could have picked that out.

Though the shift in the relationship was obvious because there was absolutely no tension that should be between a boss and his employee between us.

But there is no way someone could have deciphered or seen through our façade of normalcy just based on the fact that we became closer because that could very well be attributed to the development of trust between an employer and his employee.

Throughout the meeting hours, I had barely focused on work even though all his words of assurance were in my mind; I couldn't help but be worried about the outcome. It would be a huge disappointment if things didn't go the way he planned.

That was why I felt a wave of relief wash over me when I saw his relaxed but exhausted feature walk into my office after the meeting, I knew instantly that it went in his favor, and I was nothing but happy and proud of him.

Right now, I'm currently on his bed with my hand gently treading through his hair as he still sleeps after a passion-filled night where once again, we explored our bodies to the fullest.

I lay awake thinking about what he had said to me right after we both collapsed in exhaustion.

My mind settles on the seriousness in his eyes as he says we should no longer keep our relationship hidden from everyone.

I had been very surprised because keeping it hidden had been his idea initially, and I had completely understood his reason and went along with it.

I feel him shift as he slowly wakes up and rubs his hands on his face. He looks cute, and his tongue runs through his pink lips, wetting them all through.

I take in his morning look, a sight that doesn't fail to have an appeal to me every single time, from his drowsy eyes to his slightly parted lips to the first smile that comes to his face when he looks at me.

"Good morning, beautiful," he says to me as he places a kiss on my lips, and I smile.

"Good morning," I say with a bright smile as I place my palm on his cheek, and he turns and kisses its center with his lips tenderly.

"We should start preparing for work," he says, and I nod as he gets up from the bed and walks into the bathroom.

"Nick," I call out to him after a while, sitting up on the bed.

"Yeah?" He replies with his mouth full as he stands at the entrance to the bathroom with a toothbrush in his hand. He looks cute, and I can't help but think about the future and how I will love to see this sight for the rest of my life.

"I think we should do it today," I say to him, and he looks at me confused.

"Do what?" he asks me as he stares at me, and I sit up on the bed with a bright smile on my face as I stare at him, willing him silently to understand what I'm talking about.

"What?" he asks as he laughs at the look on my face and the general funky expression I am portraying.

"You know the thing we talked about yesterday," I say to him, and after a moment of silence, I see the expression on his face change into one of realization as he smiles at me.

"Really?" he asks with a cheery voice, and I nod repeatedly, still with a smile on my face, absolutely certain about my decision.

"Okay," He says, staring deeply into my eyes with intense emotions displayed in his.

"Okay," I say to him with my eyes mirroring the same emotions, and after a while of just simply staring at each other, an act which feels more intimate than the kiss we had shared minutes ago, he smiles and walks back into the bathroom and continues brushing.

I had concluded in my mind that as much as things are still not completely settled with him and his board, and he is willing to go down this part with me, I shouldn't hold him back; it would be nice to go on dates with him and not always have to stay in extremely private spots to avoid being seen by anyone.

Also, today is the last day of work before our Christmas break, so it wouldn't hurt so bad to be the center of attention for one day.

Though I know the pressure I would have to endure once the entire company knows about it, it will all be worth it for the growth of our relationship.

We both head to work, and I can't shake off the nerves within me at the thought of what we both are going to do today.

Once we get there, we both step down from his car, and he takes my hand and walks into the building, already sending a silent message to everyone as we receive surprised and curious stares because of our inter-joined hands, and he doesn't seem to mind, so I simply follow his lead, finding it all overwhelming.

Besides, the odds are in his favor because he is practically the boss of this company, which makes the entire thing easier for him, while I'm just an employee, so no matter how I try, I cannot settle my nerves.

"Are you okay?" he asks me once we are inside the elevator as he looks at my somewhat pale face, worried.

"Yeah. It's just overwhelming, that's all," I say to him with a smile, and he pulls me into a hug as he wraps his arms around me, slowly rubbing my back gently in a soothing manner.

"It will be okay," he says to me with a smile as he places a kiss on my forehead, and a smile comes to my face as I feel significantly better and I don't feel as worried anymore.

It's amazing how such a simple act helped calm the nerves I've been struggling with for hours.

"I love you," I say to him tenderly as I stare at him with an intense look, portraying my emotions.

I see a look of surprise come to his face at my statement, and seconds pass as he looks deeply into my eyes and smiles.

"I love you, Kat," he says to me as he leans down and kisses me deeply, as if conveying and confirming his love through a kiss.

I smile through the kiss as I return it with the same passion and emotion as the feeling of relief floods through me at his verbal assertion of reciprocated feelings.

We both end the kiss just as the elevator dings with smiles on our faces and a light and happy energy surrounding us.

Parting ways, I move speedily and set up a meeting as he had instructed me to do, a meeting that I found out happens yearly, where he addresses his staff before the close of work for the year.

In the next ten minutes, all staff are gathered in a Conference Hall and staring right at him, awaiting his speech.

"I'll make this simple and brief so that we can all return to our various responsibilities," he says with his voice exuding authority.

"Gathering from the statistics of every transaction carried out this year, this year's profit greatly surpasses last years and I have you all to thank for that. I must commend the efforts each of you have put into making sure that your various field of expertise flourishes."

"Though we lost some colleagues along the way and gained new ones also, all of you seated here managed to still keep the effective workflow in the company and this company would not be where it is without your efforts, so thank you, you are highly appreciated," he says and everyone one claps in response with wide smiles on their faces.

"To add to that, I will like to make an announcement," he starts saying, and once again, my heartbeat increases in tempo. "Miss Field please come out here," he says to me with a bright smile on his face as he stares directly at me with a hand stretched out.

All eyes turn towards me as I stand up and walk out and take his hands, returning his smile as curious looks are directed at us.

"Katrina and I are currently in an intimate relationship," he says, and I gulp lightly at his bluntness as gasps and murmurs fill the room.

"I know this comes as a shock-" he continues to say as everyone quiets down. "-but it's true," he says simply to everyone.

"Katrina, you can have your seat now," he says with a smile directed solely at me as he places a kiss on my cheek.

"In concordance with this, I'm sure you all are aware of the company's regulation regarded intimacy between employees," he says with a strict look on his face and a stern voice. "That doesn't change. That is why I'm charging you to watch us carefully, as long as we are within this buildings premises, no unethical act would be carried out between us and if any of you decide to follow in our paths, that will be allowed, but I will not hesitate relieve you of your jobs once a slip up is brought to my notice," He says with a tone of finality and everywhere is pin-drop silent.

"With that being said, Merry Christmas to everyone and a Happy New Year in advance," he says, ending his speech, and applause echoes through the hall.

After the meeting, I received a lot of statements from staff, some of congratulations and some not so pleasant, but with everything that happened today, I feel rather happy with the change.

***

NICK'S POV

I walk into my office, and not up to twenty minutes after the revelation of my relationship with Katrina, I get calls from various board members, questioning my choice to reveal my relationship, some placing complaints about the inappropriateness of my relationship, while some complaining about the stability and adherence to the regulations now that I have bridged it.

I had mentally prepared for this outcome, so for each question, I had thought up a brilliant answer in response.

Besides, this reveal just happens to be a very effective strategy to see who is against me within my board members and expunge them accordingly.

12

HAPPILY EVER AFTER

NICK'S POV

There's nothing like a well-planned party and a good woman besides you.

My dad always said when he was alive, and today I fully understand the meaning of what he said.

I look at all the guests around me, drinking, eating, and chatting merrily, and I feel a sense of pride within me at all I have been able to achieve and grateful to be where I am presently.

It's been four months since I revealed my relationship to everyone, and it has not been a smooth ride as various people tried to use that revelation as a means to rid me of my rightfully deserved inheritance.

Various forms of conflict erupted, leading to a whole lot of court cases that mostly involved me suing most of my board members for different hidden illegal crimes they committed.

Each time I took a matter to court, I always ensured that no matter how little the case, I would always come out victorious.

With each piled-up illegal act that most of my board members seemed to get involved in, it wasn't a hard course to get them all jailed.

During my expungement process, fear was driven into the heart of the remaining board members, and everyone became very cautious as not to fall on my bad side and careful not to be on my radar.

I had guaranteed that all accomplices of Mr. Saltzman that had the idea of removing both I and my brother from our positions in our company were fully expelled and totally removed from every affair that had to do with the company.

Needless to say that I had done all this with Katrina right beside me, supporting me through the entire rough phase.

"Can I have your attention, please?" Christian says as he taps his glass with a fork, bringing me out of my thoughts and drawing my focus to him.

All eyes are fixed on him as he gets on the stage and picks up a mic with his glass of wine in his hand.

"I'll make this very short, I want to propose a toast to the man of the day, a man who has worked his ass off day and night to be where he is now. A man who does ten times more work in a day than I can ever dream of doing in a year," he says in humor, and laughter fills the room, "It sounds amusing now but it's actually the truth and I wouldn't ever want to be in his shoes, all that stress can absolutely kill me," he says dramatically, and everyone laughs again, and I roll my eyes at his words.

"That being said, here's to man who toils and sweats before getting anything. To a man who holds hard work and transparency as his topmost principles. To a man who would surprise you by refusing billions of dollars if he feels he didn't work hard enough to deserve it, believe me I've seen it happen," he says, and the crowd murmurs, amused, while I glare at him, warning him to end his speech.

Usually, when he is on a roll like this, he goes on and spills embarrassing details about my life, and I honestly don't want that to happen here.

"Here's to a man who deserves to be exactly where he is today. Cheers to the new CEO of Torrent's company," he says thankfully, ending his speech, and the crowd responds and lifts their glasses.

"Why don't you come up and give us one of your famous speech, Nicky?" he asks, and I nod, going up on the stage and taking the microphone from him.

"Thank you for that very short cheer Christian," I say with sarcasm dripping from each word, referring to the first sentence he made, and everyone laughs.

He mouths 'you're welcome' silently with a huge grin on his face and walks down from the stage.

"Well, good evening everyone, I want to say simply that I appreciate all of you being here to support me during this very important stage of my life, a stage I had worked my ass off day and night for as long as Christian had said, a stage that doesn't make work easier, but requires even more effort and time. In order to keep this company afloat and prospering I promise to put in my best and ensure that I take this company to greater heights," I say.

"With all of your support and most importantly the support of a woman I've come to treasure very much, a woman who hasn't left my side ever since she found me, I believe this will be an easy task. Thank you once again, and enjoy the party," I say, and there is a round of applause as I step down from the stage.

My eyes run over the crowd looking for Katrina, whom I have not seen since this night began.

"That was a really good speech," I hear a voice say behind me, and I recognize it instantly as I turn and capture her lips in a deep kiss.

"You just happen to be its inspiration," I say with a smile which she returns with love shining in her eyes.

***

KATRINA'S POV

"So you won't tell me where we are going to," I state rather than ask Christian, who had showed up at my house with a bag and said nothing to me, playing a voice recording with Nick's voice as he instructed me to put on a short, off-shouldered flay dress that was in the bag.

A dress that, with one look, I knew was super expensive, designed with real diamonds running around the shoulder and also scattered all around the flay part of it.

I put the gown on, and the weight of it told me that Nick had definitely bought a gown with real diamonds on them for me, and if he was right in front of me, I would have scolded him for the extravagance.

"I can't tell you that Kat, I'm simply a messenger," he says simply, and I sigh.

"How am I even sure that you didn't fake that recording and you are kidnapping me to be killed?" I ask him with a glare, and he laughs.

"I wouldn't buy that gown for you if I was going to kidnap and kill you Kat," he says, and I sigh again.

"True," I say simply, and he laughs lightly again before the car falls silent as I patiently wait to get to my destination.

He turns up the radio to fill in the silence, and as the slow tune from the radio plays out, my mind goes to Nick, and I think of how far we have come together.

It's been a year since he was made the CEO of the company, and since then, work has become even more intense for him, with the only comfort being that after every two weeks of extra hard work, he takes a week's rest from meetings and works at the office.

Though he still doesn't take full advantage of this privilege and still works at home.

For the past year, the company has been flourishing, extremely so under him and our relationship has become a whole lot stronger in such a short time.

"We are here," Christian says to me as he stops the car in the middle of nowhere.

"So you actually are kidnapping me to be killed?" I ask him looking around at the very lonely road that I had been too lost in thoughts to notice we came into.

"Just come down and follow me," he sighs tiredly, but there is a smirk on his lips.

"I'm not sure if I want to," I say to him, and just as he is about to reply, he gets a call.

All I hear him say is yes and okay, and it makes this even more spooky.

"What is happening?" I ask him once he is done with his call, and he doesn't get to answer as my phone starts ringing, and I see Nick's name on the screen.

"Hey," I say as I pick up the call, not taking my eyes off Christian, who looks completely amused.

"Baby, follow Christian and come to me," He says simply and hangs up the call in a freaky way, and if I wasn't a hundred percent sure that it was his voice, I would have been completely spooked now.

Christian gets down from the car, not saying any other word, and starts walking, and I have no choice but to follow him.

We walk for a while, and I sight water, and then I realize that this is actually a beach.

I walk quietly behind him until I see lights up ahead, and he stops walking, still without saying a word ushers me with his hand to keep walking.

I oblige curiously, and I walk further down I am met with a breathtaking sight as I see Nick down on a knee with a ring in his hand, and just behind him are words shaped boldly with roses that read in capital letters-

'WILL YOU MARRY ME?'

"Katrina Fields, ever since I met you, I have known joy without no bounds, you found a way of filling me completely. You have this way of making the toughest of situations feel alright. You have been my strength, my courage's and the reason behind my happiness."

My heart begins to speed up as my hands cover my mouth. He does not stop there.

"No words can describe how much you mean to me and

how much I adore you, I love you with everything in me and I will love to have you by my side as my forever. Will you marry me?" He asks me, and I stare at him, completely stunned and speechless.

I look at the roses, and then my eyes go beyond it to see my mum, dad, my best friend, and a few other people as an audience, watching and waiting for me to reply to him.

Tears come to my eyes as I stare into the eyes of the man I love, who didn't need to say a single thing to convince me of his love for me, as the intense and loving look in his eyes says it all.

"Yes," I say happily and see his face light up in joy as he stands up and slips the ring into my finger.

Cheers erupt from behind us as we stare deeply into each other's eyes with wide smiles on our faces.

With a kiss, we seal the engagement, and at this single moment, I know that I have found my 'happily ever after.'

About the Author

J. D. Hova is an author who perfectly blends passion, hope, and real-life meanings in his romance books. When he is not writing, you can find him enjoying the great outdoors with his family, dogs, chickens, and new-born baby. J. D. believes that true love and happiness take time and his books reflect that belief. His stories capture the essence of life and offer a glimmer of hope through happy ever afters. If you enjoyed reading his books, please leave a review as he truly appreciates your feedback.

Acknowledgments

I want to take a moment to express my sincerest gratitude to all the amazing people in my life. Without the love and support of my readers, friends, family, and colleagues, I wouldn't be where I am today. I am so grateful for each and every one of you who has helped me along my path to happiness and success. I also want to give a special shoutout to those who hold me accountable and contribute so much to making this journey through life possible. And of course, I can't forget to thank the most important women who have inspired me – Linda V., my sweet baby girl Ayla, Grand Mother Louise, Mother Kathy, Sister Shannon and Aunt Christine. Thank you all from the bottom of my heart.